TO A NIGHTINGALE

Other titles by Ed Hirsch

To a Nightingale

Poems from Sappho to Borges

Edited by Edward Hirsch

GEORGE BRAZILLER PUBLISHERS / NEW YORK

PUBLICATION ACKNOWLEDGMENTS
Jorge Luis Borges' "To the Nightingale," translated by Alastair Reid. English translation copyright © 1999 by Alastair Reid. Reprinted with permission of the Thomas Colchie Agency. "Night Singing," copyright © 1996 by W.S. Merwin. Reprinted with permission of the Wylie Agency. Marie de Frances' "Laüstic," translation © 1978 by Robert Hanning and Joan Ferrante. Reprinted with permission of Baker Publishing Group.

TRANSLATION CREDITS
Ovid, "The Story of Tereus and Procne," from *Metamorphosis*, translated by Brookes More. *Rubáiyát of Omar Khayyám*, translated by Edward Fitzgerald. Sappho, "Fragments," translated by Edwin Marion Cox. Sophocles, *Oedipus at Colonus*, translated by F. Storr. Virgil, *Georgics* translated by J. W. MacKail. Petrarch, "The Song of the Nightingale Reminds Him of His Unhappy Lot," translated by Francis Wrangham. Gil Vicente, "The Nightingale," translated by John Bowring. Heinrich Heine, "New Spring" and "Book of Songs," translated by Sir Robert Randolph Garran.

Special thanks to Maxwell Heller, who made this book a reality.

For information, please address the publisher:
George Braziller, Inc.
277 Broadway, Suite 708
New York, NY 10007
www.georgebraziller.com

Library of Congress Cataloging-in-Publication Data
To a Nightingale : Poems from Sappho to Borges / edited by Edward Hirsch.—
Second edition.
        p. cm.
ISBN 978-0-8076-1627-7
1. Nightingale—Poetry. I. Hirsch, Edward, editor of compilation.
PN6110.N47T6 2013
821.008'3628—dc23   2013028564

Arranged by Linda Barney Burke, Ph.D.
Designed by Rita Lascaro
Printed in the United States of America

CONTENTS

LOVE

INTRODUCTION

It all comes down to a small, secretive, solitary songbird that goes on singing late into the night. It begins—and ends, too—with an unseen bird that continues to trill and whistle in the darkness long after the other birds have quieted for the evening. Its voice breaks the stillness. The nightingale is a common Old World bird with an uncommon sound: rich, loud, mellow, melodious. It has stamina and sings with an eerie natural beauty that reverberates like a chord through European and Asian poetry. Its song is strong and fitful—restless, compelling. It crescendoes.

The nightingale has always had tremendous metaphorical and symbolic power. It seems to fill a need—apparently irresistible—to attribute human feeling to the bird's pure and persistent song. Poets, who are often nocturnal creatures, have especially identified with "spring's messenger, the sweet-voiced nightingale," as Sappho calls it. They have also noted its difference from us. The nightingale sings during the day as well as the night, but poets have especially praised its night music, its mournful tones and its joyous sound.

In his magisterial defense of poetry, Shelley establishes the connection between the poet and the nightingale. He writes:

> A poet is a nightingale, who sits in darkness
> and sings to cheer
>   its own solitude with sweet sounds; his auditors
> are as men entranced

> by the melody of an unseen musician, who
> feel that they are moved
> and softened, yet know not whence or why.

The singing of the nightingale becomes a metaphor for writing poetry here, and listening to that bird (that natural music) becomes a metaphor for reading it. One of the Romantic premises of Shelley's metaphor is that the poet "sings" in "solitude" without any consideration for an audience and that the audience—"his auditors"—responds to the work of an "unseen musician." They are physically removed from each other, and yet they are brought into mysterious relationship.

The nightingale has often been treated as a messenger to and from the beyond, the very embodiment of a transcendent vocation. It is the most magical of songbirds. In his definitive compendium, *Shamanism*, Mircea Eliade points out that "[a]ll over the world learning the language of animals, especially of birds, is equivalent to knowing the secrets of nature and hence to being able to prophesy." He presents evidence that birdcalls can be heard during séances among the Yakut, the Yukagit, the Chukchee, the Goldi, the Inuit, and other peoples around the world. To mimic the natural call of a bird, or, more strongly, to become a bird oneself, "indicates the capacity," Eliade notes, "to undertake the ecstatic journey to the sky and beyond." It may be that a remnant of magical practice still clings to the poet who mimics the song of the nightingale.

The nightingale has its own rich history of representations in poetry. The history begins with one of the oldest legends in the world, the poignant tale of Philomela, that poor ravished girl who had her tongue cut out and was changed into the nightingale, which laments in darkness but nonetheless expresses its story in song. The tale reverberates through all of Greco-Roman literature. Ovid gave it a poignant rendering in *Metamorphosis*, and it echoes down the centuries from Shakespeare (*Titus Andronicus*) and Sidney (*O Philomela Fair*) to Matthew Arnold ("Philomela"), T. S. Eliot ("The Waste Land"), and John Crowe Ransom ("Philomela"). To listen to the nightingale and rework the story of Philomela is also a way of participating in the classical tradition. Hence Matthew Arnold's evocative address to the nightingale: "O wanderer from a Grecian shore." Whoever reads these works intensively comes away with a particular feeling—mournful, tragic—for the suffering of the hidden bird. The nightingale becomes, to use Borges's phrase, "encrusted with mythology."

The tale of Philomela mythologizes the mournful tones of the nightingale's song. To many human listeners, the nightingale seems to be crying out, whistling and gurgling, modulating its tones, expressing itself, and thereby transforming its woes into sweet sounds. Even without the mythological scrim, poets have often responded to the piercing woe-begotten quality of the nightingale's song. Petrarch gives voice to the theme:

> That nightingale, who now melodious mourns
> Perhaps his children or his consort dear,
> The heavens with sweetness fills; the distant bourns
> Resound his notes, so piteous and so clear;
> With me all night he weeps . . .

This is the tradition inherited by Charlotte Smith ("Poor

melancholy bird, that all night long/Tell'st to the moon thy tale of tender woe"), Mary Robinson ("Sweet Bird of Sorrow!"), and other Romantic poets. Christina Rossetti seems to recognize the imposition of human meaning on the nature of birdsong when she writes: "I shall not hear the nightingale/Sing on, *as if* in pain." The recognition comes in the delicate phrase "as if." With characteristic alacrity, Heine inverts the tradition by calling out:

> If the nightingales knew how ill
>   And worn with woe I be,
> They would cheerily carol and trill,
>   And all bring joy to me.

Coleridge was the first Romantic poet to attack the idea that the nightingale's song was necessarily lonesome and sad. "A melancholy Bird?" he asks in his revisionist poem "The Nightingale": "O idle thought/In nature there is nothing melancholy." There is something deeply refreshing in Coleridge's recognition that poets have gone on echoing the conceit of the nightingale's song without stretching their legs, going outside, and listening to the actual bird. "My Friend, and my Friend's Sister! we have learnt/A different lore," he declares:

> Nature's sweet voices always full of love
> And joyance! Tis the merry Nightingale
> That crowds, and hurries, and precipitates
> With fast thick warble his delicious notes,
> As if he were fearful, that an April night
> Would be too short for him to utter forth
> His love-chant, and disburthen his full soul
> Of all its music!

Coleridge also hears nightingales singing back and forth to each other ("They answer and provoke each other's songs/With skirmish and capricious passagings") and thus breaks down the convention that nightingales always sing in solitude.

Coleridge's poem is a kind of jubilant corrective to the tradition of representing nightingales sorrowfully in poetry. As a counter to the story of Philomela, poets have periodically reminded us that the nightingale is a real bird operating in the natural world. For example, the rural poet John Clare observed how nightingales actually look, sound, and behave. "I have watched them often at their song," he said. He objected to the old threadbare epithets such as "love lorn nightingale" and with a naturalist's eye remembered how assiduously he had observed one as a boy: "She is a plain bird something like the hedge sparrow in shape and the female Firetail or Redstart in color but more slender than the former and of a redder brown or scorched color than the latter." Clare loved to listen to the sounds of a nightingale and tried to transcribe its song. Here is how he describes hearing it in "The Progress of Rhyme":

> "Chew-chew chew-chew" and higher still,
> "Cheer-cheer cheer-cheer" more loud and
> shrill,
> "Cheer-up cheer-up cheer-up"—and dropped
> Low—"Tweet tweet jug jug jug"—and stopped
> One moment just to drink the sound
> Her music made, and then a round
> Of stranger witching notes was heard
> As if it was a stranger bird:
> "Wew-wew wew-wew chur-chur chur-chur
> Woo-it woo-it"—could this be her?

"Tee-rew tee-rew tee-rew tee-rew
Chew-rit chew-rit"—and ever new—
"Will-will will-will grig-grig grig-grig."

Clare's attempt to "syllable the sounds" may sound like nonsense, but it strangely captures something of the nightingale's characteristic sound and rhythm. In *Why Birds Sing* David Rothenberg calls one of Clare's verbatim descriptions "the most accurate rendering in words of any bird's voice for nearly a century."

It is in this spirit of accuracy that the Spanish poet Miguel Hernández responded to Pablo Neruda on a street in Madrid in 1934. Neruda, who was then Chile's consul to Spain, told Hernández that he had never actually heard a nightingale. It is too cold for nightingales to survive in Chile. Hernández grew up in a goatherding family in the province of Alicante, and he immediately scampered up a high tree and created the sound of a nightingale's liquid song. Then he climbed up another tree and created the sound of a second nightingale answering. He could have been joyously illustrating Boris Pasternak's notion of poetry as "two nightingales dueling."

The nightingale has an irreplaceable branch in poetry. "Thou wast not born for death, Immortal Bird!" Keats cries out at the very pinnacle of the tradition. "Perhaps I never heard you," Borges explains in his own belated ode "To the Nightingale," "but my life is bound up with your life, inseparably." So it is inevitably for each of us who love poetry. The poem about the nightingale may continually try to escape its own literary history—indeed, it needs to do so in order to stay vital—and yet it also takes its place in that splendid tradition. The tradition continually revitalizes itself by contact with an actual bird, by listening to the nightingale's song. This is the very point of W. S. Merwin's beautifully conclusive lyric "Night Singing." In the end, it all comes down to one poet listening and one small, unseen bird singing its heart out in the darkness. Its voice shatters the silence. The nightingale's song, its night singing, touches something deeply mortal—and immortal—in each of us.

Edward Hirsch

PHILOMELA: THE POET'S HERITAGE

The Tale of Tereus, Procne, and Philomela
from Ovid's Metamorphosis

The lords of many cities that were near,
now met together and implored their kings
to mourn with Pelops those unhappy deeds.—

The lords of Argos; Sparta and Mycenae;
and Calydon, before it had incurred
the hatred of Diana, goddess of the chase;
fertile Orchomenus and Corinth, great
in wealth of brass; Patrae and fierce Messena;
Cleone, small; and Pylus and Troezen,
not ruled by Pittheus then,—and also, all
the other cities which are shut off by
the Isthmus there dividing its two seas,
and all the cities which are seen from there.

What seemed most wonderful, of all those towns
Athens alone was wanting, for a war
had gathered from the distant seas, a host
of savage warriors had alarmed her walls,
and hindered her from mourning for the dead.

Now Tereus, then the mighty king of Thrace,
came to the aid of Athens as defense
from that fierce horde; and there by his great deeds
achieved a glorious fame. Since his descent
was boasted from the mighty Gradivus,
and he was gifted with enormous wealth,

Pandion, king of Athens, gave to him
in sacred wedlock his dear daughter, Procne.

But Juno, guardian of the sacred rites
attended not, nor Hymenaeus, nor
the Graces. But the Furies snatched up brands
from burning funeral pyres, and brandished them
as torches. They prepared the nuptial couch,—
a boding owl flew over the bride's room,
and then sat silently upon the roof.

With such bad omens Tereus married her,
sad Procne, and those omens cast a gloom
on all the household till the fateful birth
of their first born. All Thrace went wild with joy—
and even they, rejoicing, blessed the Gods,
when he, the little Itys, saw the light;
and they ordained each year their wedding day,
and every year the birthday of their child,
should be observed with festival and song:
so the sad veil of fate conceals from us
our future woes.

Now Titan had drawn forth
the changing seasons through five autumns, when,
in gentle accents, Procne spoke these words:
"My dearest husband, if you love me, let
me visit my dear sister, or consent
that she may come to us and promise her
that she may soon return. If you will but
permit me to enjoy her company
my heart will bless you as I bless the Gods."

At once the monarch ordered his long ships
to launch upon the sea; and driven by sail,
and hastened by the swiftly sweeping oars,
they entered the deep port of Athens, where
he made fair landing on the fortified
Piraeus. There, when time was opportune
to greet his father-in-law and shake his hand,
they both exchanged their wishes for good health,
and Tereus told the reason why he came.

He was relating all his wife's desire,
Promising Philomela's safe return
from a brief visit, when Philomela appeared
rich in her costly raiment, yet more rich
in charm and beauty, just as if a fair
Dryad or Naiad should be so attired,
appearing radiant, from dark solitudes.

As if someone should kindle whitening corn
or the dry leaves, or hay piled in a stack;
so Tereus, when he saw the beautiful
and blushing virgin, was consumed with love.

Her modest beauty was a worthy cause
of worthy love; but by his heritage,
derived from a debasing clime, his love
was base; and fires unholy burned within
from his own lawless nature, just as fierce
as are the habits of his evil race.

In the wild frenzy of his wicked heart,
he thought he would corrupt her trusted maid,
her tried attendants, and corrupt even

her virtue with large presents: he would waste
his kingdom in the effort.—He prepared
to seize her at the risk of cruel war.
And he would do or dare all things to feed
his raging flame.—He could not brook delay.

With most impassioned words he begged for her,
pretending he gave voice to Procne's hopes.—
his own desire made him wax eloquent,
as often as his words exceeded bounds,
he pleaded he was uttering Procne's words.

His hypocritic eyes were filled with tears,
as though they represented her desire—
and, O you Gods above, what devious ways
are harbored in the hearts of mortals! Through
his villainous desire he gathered praise,
and many lauded him for the great love
he bore his wife.

And even Philomela
desires her own undoing; and with fond
embraces nestles to her father, while
she pleads for his consent, that she may go
to visit her dear sister.—Tereus viewed
her pretty pleading, and in his hot heart,
imagined he was then embracing her;
and as he saw her kiss her father's lips,
her arms around his neck, it seemed that each
caress was his; and so his fire increased.
He even wished he were her father; though,
if it were so, his passion would no less
be impious.—Overcome at last by these

entreaties, her kind father gave consent.
Greatly she joyed and thanked him for her own
misfortune. She imagined a success,
instead of all the sorrow that would come.

The day declining, little of his toil
remained for Phoebus. Now his flaming steeds
were beating with their hoofs the downward slope
of high Olympus; and the regal feast
was set before the guests, and flashing wine
was poured in golden vessels, and the feast
went merrily, until the satisfied
assembly sought in gentle sleep their rest.

Not so, the love-hot Tereus, king of Thrace,
who, sleepless, imaged in his doting mind
the form of Philomela, recalled the shape
of her fair hands, and in his memory
reviewed her movements. And his flaming heart
pictured her beauties yet unseen.—He fed
his frenzy on itself, and could not sleep.

Fair broke the day; and now the ancient king,
Pandion, took his son-in-law's right hand
to bid farewell; and, as he wept,
commended his dear daughter, Philomela,
unto his guarding care. "And in your care,
my son-in-law, I trust my daughter's health.
Good reason, grounded on my love, compels
my sad approval. You have begged for her,
and both my daughters have persuaded me.
Wherefore, I do entreat you and implore
your honor, as I call upon the Gods,

that you will ever shield her with the love
of a kind father and return her safe,
as soon as may be—my last comfort given
to bless my doting age. And all delay
will agitate and vex my failing heart.

"And, O my dearest daughter, Philomela,
if you have any love for me, return
without too long delay and comfort me,
lest I may grieve; for it is quite enough
that I should suffer while your sister stays away."
The old king made them promise, and he kissed
his daughter, while he wept. Then did he join
their hands in pledge of their fidelity,
and, as he gave his blessing, cautioned them
to kiss his absent daughter and her son
for his dear sake. Then as he spoke a last
farewell, his trembling voice was filled with sobs.
And he could hardly speak;—for a great fear
from some vague intuition of his mind,
surged over him, and he was left forlorn.

So soon as Philomela was safe aboard
the painted ship and as the sailors urged
the swiftly gliding keel across the deep
and the dim land fast-faded from their view,
then Tereus, in exultant humor, thought,
"Now all is well, the object of my love
sails with me while the sailors ply the oars."

He scarcely could control his barbarous
desire—with difficulty stayed his lust,
he followed all her actions with hot eyes.—

So, when the ravenous bird of Jupiter
has caught with crooked talons the poor hare,
and dropped it—ruthless,—in his lofty nest,
where there is no escape, his cruel eyes
gloat on the victim he anticipates.

And now, as Tereus reached his journey's end,
they landed from the travel-wearied ship,
safe on the shores of his own kingdom. Then
he hastened with the frightened Philomela
into most wild and silent solitudes
of an old forest; where, concealed among
deep thickets a forbidding old house stood:
there he immured the pale and trembling maid,
who, vainly in her fright, began to call
upon her absent sister,—and her tears
implored his pity. His obdurate mind
could not be softened by such piteous cries;
but even while her agonizing screams
implored her sister's and her father's aid,
and while she vainly called upon the Gods,
he overmastered her with brutal force.—

The poor child trembled as a frightened lamb,
which, just delivered from the frothing jaws
of a gaunt wolf, dreads every moving twig.
She trembled as a timid injured dove,
(her feathers dripping with her own life-blood)
that dreads the ravening talons of a hawk
from which some fortune has delivered her.

But presently, as consciousness returned,
she tore her streaming hair and beat her arms,

and, stretching forth her hands in frenzied grief,
cried out, "Oh, barbarous and brutal wretch!
Unnatural monster of abhorrent deeds!
Could not my anxious father's parting words,
nor his foreboding tears restrain your lust?
Have you no slight regard for your chaste wife,
my dearest sister, and are you without
all honor, so to spoil virginity
now making me invade my sister's claim,
you have befouled the sacred fount of life,—
you are a lawless bond of double sin!

"Oh, this dark punishment was not my due!
Come, finish with my murder your black deed,
so nothing wicked may remain undone.
But oh, if you had only slaughtered me
before your criminal embrace befouled
my purity, I should have had a shade
entirely pure, and free from any stain!
Oh, if there is a Majesty in Heaven,
and if my ruin has not wrecked the world,
then, you shall suffer for this grievous wrong
and time shall hasten to avenge my wreck.

"I shall declare your sin before the world,
and publish my own shame to punish you!
And if I'm prisoned in the solitudes,
my voice will wake the echoes in the wood
and move the conscious rocks. Hear me, O Heaven!
And let my imprecations rouse the Gods—
ah-h-h, if there can be a god in Heaven!"

Her cries aroused the dastard tyrant's wrath,
and frightened him, lest ever his foul deed
might shock his kingdom: and, roused at once
by rage and guilty fear; he seized her hair,
forced her weak arms against her back, and bound
them fast with brazen chains, then drew his sword.

When she first saw his sword above her head.
Flashing and sharp, she wished only for death,
and offered her bare throat: but while she screamed,
and, struggling, called upon her father's name,
he caught her tongue with pincers, pitiless,

And cut it with his sword.—The mangled root
still quivered, but the bleeding tongue itself,
fell murmuring on the blood-stained floor. As the tail
of a slain snake still writhes upon the ground,
so did the throbbing tongue; and, while it died,
moved up to her, as if to seek her feet.—
And, it is said that after this foul crime,
the monster violated her again.

And after these vile deeds, that wicked king
returned to Procne, who, when she first met
her brutal husband, anxiously inquired
for tidings of her sister; but with sighs
and tears, he told a false tale of her death,
and with such woe that all believed it true.

Then Procne, full of lamentation, took
her royal robe, bordered with purest gold,
and putting it away, assumed instead
garments of sable mourning; and she built

a noble sepulchre, and offered there
her pious gifts to an imagined shade;—
lamenting the sad death of her who lived.

A year had passed by since that awful date—
the sun had coursed the Zodiac's twelve signs.
But what could Philomela hope or do?
For like a jail the strong walls of the house
were built of massive stone, and guards around
prevented flight; and mutilated, she
could not communicate with anyone
to tell her injuries and tragic woe.

But even in despair and utmost grief,
there is an ingenuity which gives
inventive genius to protect from harm:
and now, the grief-distracted Philomela
wove in a warp with purple marks and white,
a story of the crime; and when 'twas done
she gave it to her one attendant there
and begged her by appropriate signs to take
it secretly to Procne. She took the web,
she carried it to Procne, with no thought
of words or messages by art conveyed.

The wife of that inhuman tyrant took
the cloth, and after she unwrapped it saw
and understood the mournful record sent.
She pondered it in silence and her tongue
could find no words to utter her despair;—
her grief and frenzy were too great for tears.—
In a mad rage her rapid mind counfounded
the right and wrong—intent upon revenge.

Since it was now the time of festival,
when all the Thracian matrons celebrate
the rites of Bacchus—every third year thus—
night then was in their secret; and at night
the slopes of Rhodope resounded loud
with clashing of shrill cymbals. So, at night
the frantic queen of Tereus left her home
and, clothed according to the well known rites
of Bacchus, hurried to the wilderness.

Her head was covered with the green vine leaves;
and from her left side native deer skin hung;
and on her shoulder rested a light spear.—
so fashioned, the revengeful Procne rushed
through the dark woods, attended by a host
of screaming followers, and wild with rage,
pretended it was Bacchus urged her forth.

At last she reached the lonely building, where
her sister, Philomela, was immured;
and as she howled and shouted "Ee-woh-ee-e!,"
She forced the massive doors; and having seized
her sister, instantly concealed her face
in ivy leaves, arrayed her in the trappings
of Bacchanalian rites. When this was done,
they rushed from there, demented, to the house
where as the Queen of Tereus, Procne dwelt.

When Philomela knew she had arrived
at that accursed house, her countenance,
though pale with grief, took on a ghastlier hue:
and, wretched in her misery and fright,
she shuddered in convulsions.—Procne took

the symbols, Bacchanalian, from her then,
and as she held her in a strict embrace
unveiled her downcast head. But she refused
to lift her eyes, and fixing her sad gaze
on vacant space, she raised her hand, instead;
as if in oath she called upon the Gods
to witness truly she had done no wrong,
but suffered a disgrace of violence.—

Lo, Procne, wild with a consuming rage,
cut short her sister's terror in these words,
"This is no time for weeping! awful deeds
demand a great revenge—take up the sword,
and any weapon fiercer than its edge!
My breast is hardened to the worst of crime
make haste with me! together let us put
this palace to the torch!

"Come, let us maim,
the beastly Tereus with revenging iron,
cut out his tongue, and quench his cruel eyes,
and hurl and burn him writhing in the flames!
Or, shall we pierce him with a grisly blade,
and let his black soul issue from deep wounds
a thousand.—Slaughter him with every death
imagined in the misery of hate!"

While Procne still was raving out such words,
Itys, her son, was hastening to his mother;
and when she saw him, her revengeful eyes
conceiving a dark punishment, she said,
"Aha! here comes the image of his father!"

She gave no other warning, but prepared
to execute a horrible revenge.

But when the tender child came up to her,
and called her "mother," put his little arms
around her neck, and when he smiled and kissed
her often, gracious in his cunning ways,—
again the instinct of true motherhood
pulsed in her veins, and moved to pity, she
began to weep in spite of her resolve.

Feeling the tender impulse of her love
unnerving her, she turned her eyes from him
and looked upon her sister, and from her
glanced at her darling boy again. And so,
while she was looking at them both, by turns,
she said, "Why does the little one prevail
with pretty words, while Philomela stands
in silence always, with her tongue torn out?
She cannot call her sister, whom he calls
his mother! Oh, you daughter of Pandion,
consider what a wretch your husband is!
The wife of such a monster must be flint;
compassion in her heart is but a crime."

No more she hesitated, but as swift
as the fierce tigress of the Ganges leaps,
seizes the suckling offspring of the hind,
and drags it through the forest to its lair;
so, Procne seized and dragged the frightened boy
to a most lonely section of the house;
and there she put him to the cruel sword,
while he, aware of his sad fate, stretched forth

his little hands, and cried, "Ah, mother,—ah!—"
And clung to her—clung to her, while she struck—
her fixed eyes, maddened, glaring horribly—
struck wildly, lopping off his tender limbs.
But Philomela cut through his tender throat.

Then they together, mangled his remains,
still quivering with the remnant of his life,
and boiled a part of him in steaming pots,
that bubbled over with the dead child's blood,
and roasted other parts on hissing spits.

And, after all was ready, Procne bade
her husband, Tereus, to the loathsome feast,
and with a false pretense of sacred rites,
according to the custom of her land,
by which, but one man may partake of it,
she sent the servants from the banquet hall.—
Tereus, majestic on his ancient throne
high in imagined state, devoured his son,
and gorged himself with flesh of his own flesh—
and in his rage of gluttony called out
for Itys to attend and share the feast!

Curst with a joy she could conceal no more,
and eager to gloat over his distress,
Procne cried out,

"Inside yourself, you have
the thing that you are asking for!"—Amazed,
he looked around and called his son again:—

that instant, Philomela sprang forth—her hair
disordered, and all stained with blood of murder,
unable then to speak, she hurled the head
of Itys in his father's fear-struck face,
and more than ever longed for fitting words.

The Thracian Tereus overturned the table,
and howling, called up from the Stygian pit,
the viperous sisters. Tearing at his breast,
in miserable efforts to disgorge
the half-digested gobbets of his son,
he called himself his own child's sepulchre,
and wept the hot tears of a frenzied man.
Then with his sword he rushed at the two sisters.

Fleeing from him, they seemed to rise on wings,
and it was true, for they had changed to birds.
Then Philomela, flitting to the woods,
found refuge in the leaves: but Procne flew
straight to the sheltering gables of a roof—
and always, if you look, you can observe
the brand of murder on the swallow's breast—
red feathers from that day. And Tereus, swift
in his great agitation, and his will
to wreak a fierce revenge, himself is turned
into a crested bird. His long, sharp beak
is given him instead of a long sword,
and so, because his beak is long and sharp,
he rightly bears the name of Hoopoe.

Ode to a Nightingale

JOHN KEATS

My heart aches, and a drowsy numbness pains
   My sense, as though of hemlock I had drunk,
Or emptied some dull opiate to the drains
   One minute past, and Lethe-wards had sunk:
'Tis not through envy of thy happy lot,
   But being too happy in thine happiness,—
      That thou, light-wingèd Dryad of the trees
        In some melodious plot
   Of beechen green, and shadows numberless,
      Singest of summer in full-throated ease.

O, for a draught of vintage! that hath been
   Cool'd a long age in the deep-delvèd earth,
Tasting of Flora and the country green,
   Dance, and Provençal song, and sunburnt mirth!
O for a beaker full of the warm South,
   Full of the true, the blushful Hippocrene,
      With beaded bubbles winking at the brim,
        And purple-stainèd mouth;
   That I might drink, and leave the world unseen,
      And with thee fade away into the forest dim:

Fade far away, dissolve, and quite forget
   What thou among the leaves hast never known,
The weariness, the fever, and the fret
   Here, where men sit and hear each other groan;
Where palsy shakes a few, sad, last gray hairs,
   Where youth grows pale, and spectre-thin, and dies;
      Where but to think is to be full of sorrow

And leaden-eyed despairs,
 Where Beauty cannot keep her lustrous eyes,
  Or new Love pine at them beyond to-morrow.

Away! away! for I will fly to thee,
 Not charioted by Bacchus and his pards,
But on the viewless wings of Poesy,
 Though the dull brain perplexes and retards:
Already with thee! tender is the night,
 And haply the Queen-Moon is on her throne,
  Cluster'd around by all her starry Fays;
   But here there is no light,
 Save what from heaven is with the breezes blown
  Through verdurous glooms and winding mossy ways.

I cannot see what flowers are at my feet,
 Nor what soft incense hangs upon the boughs,
But, in embalmèd darkness, guess each sweet
 Wherewith the seasonable month endows
The grass, the thicket, and the fruit-tree wild;
 White hawthorn, and the pastoral eglantine;
  Fast fading violets cover'd up in leaves;
   And mid-May's eldest child,
 The coming musk-rose, full of dewy wine,
  The murmurous haunt of flies on summer eves.

Darkling I listen; and, for many a time
 I have been half in love with easeful Death,
Call'd him soft names in many a musèd rhyme,
 To take into the air my quiet breath;
Now more than ever seems it rich to die,
 To cease upon the midnight with no pain,
  While thou art pouring forth thy soul abroad

In such an ecstasy!
Still wouldst thou sing, and I have ears in vain—
To thy high requiem become a sod.

Thou wast not born for death, immortal Bird!
No hungry generations tread thee down;
The voice I hear this passing night was heard
In ancient days by emperor and clown:
Perhaps the self-same song that found a path
Through the sad heart of Ruth, when, sick for home,
She stood in tears amid the alien corn;
The same that oft-times hath
Charm'd magic casements, opening on the foam
Of perilous seas, in faery lands forlorn.

Forlorn! the very word is like a bell
To toll me back from thee to my sole self!
Adieu! the fancy cannot cheat so well
As she is fam'd to do, deceiving elf.
Adieu! adieu! thy plaintive anthem fades
Past the near meadows, over the still stream,
Up the hill-side; and now 'tis buried deep
In the next valley-glades:
Was it a vision, or a waking dream?
Fled is that music:—Do I wake or sleep?

Canto the Second
from The Prophecy of Dante

GEORGE GORDON, LORD BYRON

But I will make another tongue arise
    As lofty and more sweet, in which expressed
  The hero's ardour, or the lover's sighs,
    Shall find alike such sounds for every theme
    That every word, as brilliant as thy skies,
  Shall realise a Poet's proudest dream,
    And make thee Europe's Nightingale of Song;
    So that all present speech to thine shall seem
The note of meaner birds, and every tongue
    Confess its barbarism when compared with thine.

Philomela

MATTHEW ARNOLD

Hark! ah, the nightingale—
The tawny-throated!
Hark, from that moonlit cedar what a burst!
What triumph! hark!—what pain!

O wanderer from a Grecian shore,
Still, after many years, in distant lands,
Still nourishing in thy bewilder'd brain
That wild, unquench'd, deep-sunken, old-world pain—
Say, will it never heal?
And can this fragrant lawn
With its cool trees, and night,
And the sweet, tranquil Thames,
And moonshine, and the dew,
To thy rack'd heart and brain
Afford no balm?

Dost thou to-night behold,
Here, through the moonlight on this English grass,
The unfriendly palace in the Thracian wild?
Dost thou again peruse
With hot cheeks and sear'd eyes
The too clear web, and thy dumb sister's shame?
Dost thou once more assay
Thy flight, and feel come over thee,
Poor fugitive, the feathery change
Once more, and once more seem to make resound
With love and hate, triumph and agony,
Lone Daulis, and the high Cephissian vale?

Listen, Eugenia—
How thick the bursts come crowding through the leaves!
Again—thou hearest?
Eternal passion!
Eternal pain!

Critic and Poet: An Apologue

Emma Lazarus

("Poetry must be simple, sensuous, or impassioned;
this man is neither simple, sensuous, nor impassioned;
therefore he is not a poet.")

No man had ever heard a nightingale,
When once a keen-eyed naturalist was stirred
To study and define—what is a bird,
To classify by rote and book, nor fail
To mark its structure and to note the scale
Whereon its song might possibly be heard.
Thus far, no farther;—so he spake the word.
When of a sudden,—hark, the nightingale!

Oh deeper, higher than he could divine
That all-unearthly, untaught strain! He saw
The plain, brown warbler, unabashed. "Not mine"
(He cried) "the error of this fatal flaw.
No bird is this, it soars beyond my line,
Were it a bird, 't would answer to my law."

Sweeney Among the Nightingales

T.S. ELIOT

"Alas, I am struck with a mortal blow within."
                    —Aeschylus, *Agamemnon*

Apeneck Sweeney spreads his knees
Letting his arms hang down to laugh,
The zebra stripes along his jaw
Swelling to maculate giraffe.

The circles of the stormy moon
Slide westward toward the River Plate,
Death and the Raven drift above
And Sweeney guards the hornèd gate.

Gloomy Orion and the Dog
Are veiled; and hushed the shrunken seas;
The person in the Spanish cape
Tries to sit on Sweeney's knees

Slips and pulls the tablecloth
Overturns a coffee cup,
Reorganized upon the floor
She yawns and draws a stocking up;

The silent man in mocha brown
Sprawls at the window sill and gapes;
The waiter brings in oranges
Bananas figs and hothouse grapes;

The silent vertebrate in brown
Contracts and concentrates, withdraws;
Rachel née Rabinovitch
Tears at the grapes with murderous paws;

She and the lady in the cape
Are suspect, thought to be in league;
Therefore the man with heavy eyes
Declines the gambit, shows fatigue,

Leaves the room and reappears
Outside the window, leaning in,
Branches of wistaria
Circumscribe a golden grin;

The host with someone indistinct
Converses at the door apart,
The nightingales are singing near
The Convent of the Sacred Heart,

And sang within the bloody wood
When Agamemnon cried aloud,
And let their liquid siftings fall
To stain the stiff dishonored shroud.

from Wastleland

T.S. ELIOT

Above the antique mantel was displayed
As though a window gave upon the sylvan scene
The change of Philomel, by the barbarous king
So rudely forced; yet there the nightingale
Filled all the desert with inviolable voice
And still she cried, and still the world pursues,
"Jug Jug" to dirty ears.

To The Nightingale

Jorge Luis Borges

Out of what secret English summer evening
or night on the incalculable Rhine,
lost among all the nights of my long night,
could it have come to my unknowing ear,
your song, encrusted with mythology,
nightingale of Virgil and the Persians?
Perhaps I never heard you, but my life
is bound up with your life, inseparably.
The symbol for you was a wandering spirit
in a book of enigmas. The poet, El Marino,
nicknamed you the "siren of the forest";
you sing throughout the night of Juliet
and through the intricate pages of the Latin
and from his pinewoods, Heine, that other
nightingale of Germany and Judea,
called you mockingbird, firebird, bird of mourning.
Keats heard your song for everyone, forever.
There is not one among the shimmering names
people have given you across the earth
that does not seek to match your own music,
nightingale of the dark. The Muslim dreamed you
in the delirium of ecstasy,
his breast pierced by the thorn of the sung rose
you redden with your blood. Assiduously
in the black evening I contrive this poem,
nightingale of the sands and all the seas,
that in exultation, memory, and fable,
you burn with love and die in liquid song.

Night Singing

W. S. MERWIN

Long after Ovid's story of Philomela
    has gone out of fashion and after the testimonials
of Hafiz and Keats have been smothered in comment
    and droned dead in schools and after Eliot has gone
    home
from the Sacred Heart and Ransom has spat and consigned
    to human youth what he reduced to fairy numbers
after the name has become slightly embarrassing
    and dried skins have yielded their details and tapes
    have been
slowed and analyzed and there is nothing at all
    for me to say one nightingale is singing
nearby in the oaks where I can see nothing but darkness
    and can only listen and ride out on the long note's
invisible beam that wells and bursts up from its
    unknown star on on on and never returning
never the same never caught while through the small leaves
    of May the starlight glitters from its own journeys
once in the ancestry of this song my mother visited here
    lightning struck the locomotive in the mountains
it had never happened before and there were so many
    things to tell that she had seen and she would never
have imagined now a field away I hear another
    voice beginning and on the slopes there is a third
not echoing but varying after the lives
    after the good-byes after the faces and the light
after the recognitions and the touching and tears
    those voices go on rising if I knew I would hear
in the last dark that singing I know how I would listen.

JOY

from Sappho's Fragments

SAPPHO

The messenger of spring, the sweet voiced nightingale.

from Oedipus at Colonus

SOPHOCLES

Thou hast come to a steed-famed land for rest,
O stranger worn with toil,
To a land of all lands the goodliest
Colonus' glistening soil.
'Tis the haunt of the clear-voiced nightingale,
Who hid in her bower, among
The wine-dark ivy that wreathes the vale,
Trilleth her ceaseless song;
And she loves, where the clustering berries nod
O'er a sunless, windless glade,
The spot by no mortal footstep trod,
The pleasance kept for the Bacchic god,
Where he holds each night his revels wild
With the nymphs who fostered the lusty child.

from The Rubáiyát of Omar Khayyám

Omar Khayyám

And David's Lips are locked; but in divine
High piping Pehlevi, with "Wine! Wine! Wine!
Red Wine!"—the Nightingale cries to the Rose
That sallow Cheek of hers to incarnadine.

from The Rose Has Flushed Red

HAFIZ

The rose has flushed red, the bud has burst,
And drunk with joy is the nightingale
Hail, Sufis! lovers of wine all hail!
For wine is proclaimed to a world athirst
Like a rock your repentance seemed to you;
Behold the marvel! of what avail
Was your rock, for a goblet has cleft it in two!

from The Merchant of Venice

WILLIAM SHAKESPEARE

The crow doth sing as sweetly as the lark,
When neither is attended, and I think
The nightingale, if she should sing by day,
When every goose is cackling, would be thought
No better a musician than the wren.
How many things by season season'd are
To their right praise and true perfection!

from Romeo and Juliet

WILLIAM SHAKESPEARE

Juliet: Wilt thou be gone? It is not yet near day.
It was the nightingale, and not the lark,
That pierc'd the fearful hollow of thine ear.
Nightly she sings on yond pomegranate tree.
Believe me, love, it was the nightingale.

Romeo: It was the lark, the herald of the morn;
No nightingale. Look, love, what envious streaks
Do lace the severing clouds in yonder East.
Night's candles are burnt out, and jocund day
Stands tiptoe on the misty mountain tops.
I must be gone and live, or stay and die.

from The Two Gentlemen of Verona

WILLIAM SHAKESPEARE

And why not death rather than living torment?
To die is to be banish'd from myself;
And Silvia is myself: banish'd from her
Is self from self: a deadly banishment!
What light is light, if Silvia be not seen?
What joy is joy, if Silvia be not by?
Unless it be to think that she is by
And feed upon the shadow of perfection.
Except I be by Silvia in the night,
There is no music in the nightingale . . .

from The Second Dayes Lamentation of the Affectionate Shepheard

RICHARD BARNFIELD

And yet the silver-noted nightingale,
Though she be not so white, is more esteemed;
Sturgion is dun of hew, white is the whale,
Yet for the daintier dish the first is deemed:
What thing is whiter than the milke-bred lilly?
That knowes it not for naught, what man so silly?

The Nightingale

Samuel Taylor Coleridge

No cloud, no relique of the sunken day
Distinguishes the West, no long thin slip
Of sullen Light, no obscure trembling hues.
Come, we will rest on this old mossy Bridge!
You see the glimmer of the stream beneath,
But hear no murmuring: it flows silently
O'er its soft bed of verdure. All is still,
A balmy night! and tho' the stars be dim,
Yet let us think upon the vernal showers
That gladden the green earth, and we shall find
A pleasure in the dimness of the stars.
And hark! the Nightingale begins its song,
"Most musical, most melancholy"
A melancholy Bird? O idle thought!
In nature there is nothing melancholy.
—But some night-wandering Man, whose heart was pierc'd
With the remembrance of a grievous wrong,
Or slow distemper or neglected love,
(And so, poor Wretch! fill'd all things with himself
And made all gentle sounds tell back the tale
Of his own sorrows) he and such as he
First nam'd these notes a melancholy strain;
And many a poet echoes the conceit,
Poet, who hath been building up the rhyme
When he had better far have stretch'd his limbs
Beside a brook in mossy forest-dell
By sun or moonlight, to the influxes
Of shapes and sounds and shifting elements
Surrendering his whole spirit, of his song

And of his fame forgetful! so his fame
Should share in nature's immortality,
A venerable thing! and so his song
Should make all nature lovelier, and itself
Be lov'd, like nature!—But 'twill not be so;
And youths and maidens most poetical
Who lose the deep'ning twilights of the spring
In ball-rooms and hot theatres, they still
Full of meek sympathy must heave their sighs
O'er Philomela's pity-pleading strains.
My Friend, and my Friend's Sister! we have learnt
A different lore: we may not thus profane
Nature's sweet voices always full of love
And joyance! 'Tis the merry Nightingale
That crowds, and hurries, and precipitates
With fast thick warble his delicious notes,
As he were fearful, that an April night
Would be too short for him to utter forth
His love-chant, and disburthen his full soul
Of all its music! And I know a grove
Of large extent, hard by a castle huge
Which the great lord inhabits not: and so
This grove is wild with tangling underwood,
And the trim walks are broken up, and grass,
Thin grass and king-cups grow within the paths.
But never elsewhere in one place I knew
So many Nightingales: and far and near
In wood and thicket over the wide grove
They answer and provoke each other's songs—
With skirmish and capricious passagings,
And murmurs musical and swift jug jug
And one low piping sound more sweet than all—
Stirring the air with such an harmony,

That should you close your eyes, you might almost
Forget it was not day! On moonlight bushes,
Whose dewy leaflets are but half disclos'd,
You may perchance behold them on the twigs,
Their bright, bright eyes, their eyes both bright and full,
Glist'ning, while many a glow-worm in the shade
Lights up her love-torch.

A most gentle Maid
Who dwelleth in her hospitable home
Hard by the castle, and at latest eve,
(Even like a Lady vow'd and dedicate
To something more than Nature in the grove)
Glides thro' the pathways; she knows all their notes,
That gentle Maid! and oft, a moment's space,
What time the moon was lost behind a cloud,
Hath heard a pause of silence: till the moon
Emerging, hath awaken'd earth and sky
With one sensation, and those wakeful birds
Have all burst forth in choral minstrelsy,
As if one quick and sudden gale had swept
An hundred airy harps! And she hath watch'd
Many a Nightingale perch giddily
On blos'my twig still swinging from the breeze,
And to that motion tune his wanton song,
Like tipsy Joy that reels with tossing head.

Farewell, O Warbler! till to-morrow eve,
And you, my friends! farewell, a short farewell!
We have been loitering long and pleasantly,
And now for our dear homes.—That strain again!
Full fain it would delay me!—My dear Babe,
Who, capable of no articulate sound,

Mars all things with his imitative lisp,
How he would place his hand beside his ear,
His little hand, the small forefinger up,
And bid us listen! And I deem it wise
To make him Nature's playmate. He knows well
The evening star: and once when he awoke
In most distressful mood (some inward pain
Had made up that strange thing, an infant's dream)
I hurried with him to our orchard plot,
And he beholds the moon, and hush'd at once
Suspends his sobs, and laughs most silently,
While his fair eyes that swam with undropped tears
Did glitter in the yellow moon-beam! Well—
It is a father's tale. But if that Heaven
Should give me life, his childhood shall grow up
Familiar with these songs, that with the night
He may associate Joy! Once more farewell,
Sweet Nightingale! once more, my friends! farewell.

from Prometheus Unbound

PERCY BYSSHE SHELLEY

There the voluptuous nightingales,
    Are awake through all the broad noonday.
When one with bliss or sadness fails,
       And through the windless ivy-boughs,
    Sick with sweet love, droops dying away
On its mate's music-panting bosom;
Another from the swinging blossom,
       Watching to catch the languid close
    Of the last strain, then lifts on high
    The wings of the weak melody,
'Till some new strain of feeling bear
    The song, and all the woods are mute;
When there is heard through the dim air
The rush of wings, and rising there
    Like many a lake-surrounded flute,
Sounds overflow the listener's brain
So sweet, that joy is almost pain.

The Woodman and The Nightingale

Percy Bysshe Shelley

A woodman whose rough heart was out of tune
(I think such hearts yet never came to good)
Hated to hear, under the stars or moon,

One nightingale in an interfluous wood
Satiate the hungry dark with melody;—
And as a vale is watered by a flood,

Or as the moonlight fills the open sky
Struggling with darkness—as a tuberose
Peoples some Indian dell with scents which lie

Like clouds above the flower from which they rose,
The singing of that happy nightingale
In this sweet forest, from the golden close

Of evening till the star of dawn may fail,
Was interfused upon the silentness;
The folded roses and the violets pale

Heard her within their slumbers, the abyss
Of heaven with all its planets; the dull ear
Of the night-cradled earth; the loneliness

Of the circumfluous waters,—every sphere
And every flower and beam and cloud and wave,
And every wind of the mute atmosphere,

And every beast stretched in its rugged cave,
And every bird lulled on its mossy bough,
And every silver moth fresh from the grave

Which is its cradle—ever from below
Aspiring like one who loves too fair, too far,
To be consumed within the purest glow

Of one serene and unapproachèd star,
As if it were a lamp of earthly light,
Unconscious, as some human lovers are,

Itself how low, how high beyond all height
The heaven where it would perish!—and every form
That worshipped in the temple of the night

Was awed into delight, and by the charm
Girt as with an interminable zone,
Whilst that sweet bird, whose music was a storm

Of sound, shook forth the dull oblivion
Out of their dreams; harmony became love
In every soul but one.

———•◦•◦•———

And so this man returned with axe and saw
At evening close from killing the tall treen,
The soul of whom by Nature's gentle law

Was each a wood-nymph, and kept ever green
The pavement and the roof of the wild copse,
Chequering the sunlight of the blue serene

With jagged leaves,—and from the forest tops
Singing the winds to sleep—or weeping oft
Fast showers of areal water-drops

Into their mother's bosom, sweet and soft,
Nature's pure tears which have no bitterness;—
Around the cradles of the birds aloft

They spread themselves into the loveliness
Of fan-like leaves, and over pallid flowers
Hang like moist clouds:—or, where high branches kiss,

Make a green space among the silent bowers,
Like a vast fane in a metropolis,
Surrounded by the columns and the towers

All overwrought with branch-like traceries
In which there is religion—and the mute
Persuasion of unkindled melodies,

Odours and gleams and murmurs, which the lute
Of the blind pilot-spirit of the blast
Stirs as it sails, now grave and now acute,

Wakening the leaves and waves, ere it has passed
To such brief unison as on the brain
One tone, which never can recur, has cast,
One accent never to return again.

The world is full of Woodmen who expel
Love's gentle Dryads from the haunts of life,
And vex the nightingales in every dell.

Twilight Calm

CHRISTINA ROSSETTI

Hark! that's the nightingale,
Telling the selfsame tale
Her song told when this ancient earth was young:
So echoes answered when her song was sung
In the first wooded vale.

We call it love and pain
The passion of her strain;
And yet we little understand or know:
Why should it not be rather joy that so
Throbs in each throbbing vein?

SORROW

from The Georgics

VIRGIL

Seven whole months unbroken they say he wept alone beneath an aëry rock by Strymon's solitary wave, and poured forth all his tale under the freezing stars, soothing tigresses and moving oaks with song: even as the nightingale mourning under the poplar shade moans her lost brood whom the cruel ploughman has marked and torn unfledged from the nest: but she weeps nightlong, and seated on the bough renews her pitiable song and fills the region round with her mournful complaint.

The Song of the Nightingale Reminds him of his Unhappy Lot

PETRARCH

Yon nightingale, whose bursts of thrilling tone,
Pour'd in soft sorrow from her tuneful throat,
Haply her mate or infant brood bemoan,
Filling the fields and skies with pity's note;
Here lingering till the long long night is gone,
Awakes the memory of my cruel lot—
But I my wretched self must wail alone:
Fool, who secure from death an angel thought!
O easy duped, who thus on hope relies!
Who would have deem'd the darkness, which appears,
From orbs more brilliant than the sun should rise?
Now know I, made by sad experience wise,
That Fate would teach me by a life of tears,
On wings how fleeting fast all earthly rapture flies!

Yon nightingale, whose strain so sweetly flows,
Mourning her ravish'd young or much-loved mate,
A soothing charm o'er all the valleys throws
And skies, with notes well tuned to her sad state:
And all the night she seems my kindred woes
With me to weep and on my sorrows wait;
Sorrows that from my own fond fancy rose,
Who deem'd a goddess could not yield to fate.
How easy to deceive who sleeps secure!
Who could have thought that to dull earth would turn
Those eyes that as the sun shone bright and pure?

Ah! now what Fortune wills I see full sure:
That loathing life, yet living I should see
How few its joys, how little they endure!

That nightingale, who now melodious mourns
Perhaps his children or his consort dear,
The heavens with sweetness fills; the distant bourns
Resound his notes, so piteous and so clear;
With me all night he weeps, and seems by turns
To upbraid me with my fault and fortune drear,
Whose fond and foolish heart, where grief sojourns,
A goddess deem'd exempt from mortal fear.
Security, how easy to betray!
The radiance of those eyes who could have thought
Should e'er become a senseless clod of clay?
Living, and weeping, late I've learn'd to say
That here below—Oh, knowledge dearly bought!—
Whate'er delights will scarcely last a day!
The radiance of those eyes who could have thought
Should e'er become a senseless clod of clay?
Living, and weeping, late I've learn'd to say
That here below—Oh, knowledge dearly bought!—
Whate'er delights will scarcely last a day!

from Here Will I Take My Rest

HAFIZ

Dear were the days which perished with my friend—
Ah, what is left of life, now she is dead,
All wisdomless and profitless I spend!
The nightingale his own life's blood doth shed,
When, to the kisses of the wind, the morn
Unveils the rose's splendour—with his torn
And jealous breast he dyes her petals red.

The Nightingale

GIL VICENTE

The rose looks out in the valley
And thither will I go!
To the rosy vale where the nightingale
Sings his song of woe.

The virgin is on the river-side
Culling the lemons pale;
Thither,—yes! thither will I go
To the rosy vale where the nightingale
Sings his song of woe.

The fairest fruit her hand hath culled,
'Tis for her lover all,
Thither,—yes! thither will I go
To the rosy vale where the nightingale
Sings his song of woe.

In her hat of straw, for her gentle swain,
She has placed the lemons pale;
Thither,—yes! thither will I go
To the rosy vale where the nightingale
Sings his song of woe.

from The Two Gentlemen of Verona

William Shakespeare

How use doth breed a habit in a man!
This shadowy desert, unfrequented woods,
I better brook than flourishing peopled towns:
Here can I sit alone, unseen of any,
And to the nightingale's complaining notes
Tune my distresses and record my woes.

Song *from* O Philomela Fair

To the tune of "Non credo gia che piu infelice amante."

SIR PHILIP SIDNEY

I.

The nightingale, as soon as April bringeth
Unto her rested sense a perfect waking,
While late bare earth, proud of new clothing, springeth,
Sings out her woes, a thorn her song-book making;
And mournfully bewailing,
Her throat in tunes expresseth
What grief her breast oppresseth,
For Tereus' force on her chaste will prevailing.

O Philomela fair! O take some gladness,
That here is juster cause of plaintful sadness:
Thine earth now springs, mine fadeth;
Thy thorn without, my thorn my heart invadeth.

II.

Alas! she hath no other cause of anguish,
But Tereus' love, on her by strong hand wroken,
Wherein she suffering, all her spirits languish,
Full womanlike, complains her will was broken,
But I, who daily craving,
Cannot have to content me,
Have more cause to lament me,
Since wanting is more woe than too much having.

O Philomela fair! O take some gladness,
That here is juster cause of plaintful sadness:
Thine earth now springs, mine fadeth;
Thy thorn without, my thorn my heart invadeth.

Sonnet to a Nightingale

Charlotte Turner Smith

Sonnet LV

POOR melancholy bird, that all night long
Tell'st to the moon thy tale of tender woe;
From what sad cause can such sweet sorrow flow,
And whence this mournful melody of song?

Thy poet's musing fancy would translate
What mean the sounds that swell thy little breast,
When still at dewy eve thou leav'st thy nest,
Thus to the listening night to sing thy fate.

Pale Sorrow's victims wert thou once among,
Tho' now releas'd in woodlands wild to rove,
Or hast thou felt from friends some cruel wrong,
Or diedst thou martyr of disastrous love?
Ah! songstress sad! that such my lot might be,
To sigh and sing at liberty—like thee!

Ode to the Nightingale

MARY ROBINSON

SWEET BIRD OF SORROW!—why complain
     In such soft melody of Song,
That ECHO, am'rous of thy Strain,
     The ling'ring cadence doth prolong?
Ah! tell me, tell me, why,
Thy dulcet Notes ascend the sky.
Or on the filmy vapours glide
Along the misty moutain's side?
And wherefore dost Thou love to dwell,
In the dark wood and moss-grown cell,
Beside the willow-margin'd stream—
Why dost Thou court wan Cynthia's beam?
Sweet Songstress—if thy wayward fate
Hath robb'd Thee of thy bosom's mate,
Oh, think not thy heart-piercing moan
     Evap'rates on the breezy air,

     Or that the plaintive Song of Care
Steals from thy Widow'd Breast alone.
Oft have I heard thy mournful Tale,
On the high Cliff, that o'er the Vale
Hangs its dark brow, whose awful shade
Spreads a deep gloom along the glade:
Led by its sound, I've wander'd far,
Till crimson evening's flaming Star
On Heav'n's vast dome refulgent hung,
And round ethereal vapours flung;
And oft I've sought th'HYGEIAN MAID,
In rosy dimply smiles array'd,

Till forc'd with every HOPE to part,
Resistless Pain subdued my Heart.

Oh then, far o'er the restless deep
      Forlorn my poignant pangs I bore,
Alone in foreign realms to weep,
      Where ENVY's voice could taunt no more.
I hop'd, by mingling with the gay,
To snatch the veil of Grief away;
To break Affliction's pond'rous chain;
VAIN was the Hope—in vain I sought
The placid hour of careless thought,
Where Fashion wing'd her light career,
      And sportive Pleasure danc'd along,
      Oft have I shunn'd the blithesome throng,
To hide th'involuntary tear,
        For e'en where rapt'rous transports glow,
From the full Heart the conscious tear will flow,

    When to my downy couch remov'd,
      FANCY recall'd my wearied mind
      To scenes of FRIENDSHIP left behind,
Scenes still regretted, still belov'd!
Ah, then I felt the pangs of Grief,
Grasp my warm Heart, and mock relief;
My burning lids Sleep's balm defied,
And on my fev'rish lip imperfect murmurs died.

    Restless and sad—I sought once more
    A calm retreat on BRITAIN's shore;
    Deceitful HOPE, e'en there I found
      That soothing FRIENDSHIP's specious name

Was but a short-liv'd empty sound,
	And LOVE a false delusive flame.

Then come, Sweet BIRD, and with thy strain,
Steal from my breast the thorn of pain;
Blest solace of my lonely hours,
In craggy caves and silent bow'rs,
When HAPPY Mortals seek repose,
By Night's pale lamp we'll chaunt our woes,
And, as her chilling tears diffuse
O'er the white thorn their silv'ry dews,
I'll with the lucid boughs entwine
	A weeping Wreath, which round my Head
Shall by the waning Crescent shine,
	And light us to our leafy bed,—
But ah! nor leafy beds nor bow'rs
Fring'd with soft MAY's enamell'd flow'rs,

Nor pearly leaves, nor Cynthia's beams,
Nor smiling Pleasure's shad'wy dreams,
	Sweet BIRD, not e'en THY melting Strains
Can calm the Heart, where TYRANT SORROW REIGNS.

from New Spring

Heinrich Heine

Nightingale! I hear thee also,
    Piping blissful-sad and lonely,
Sobbing tones and long-protracted,
    And thy song of love is only!

——◆•◆•◆——

The beauteous eyes of spring's fair night,
    With comfort are downward gazing:
If love hath made thee so small in our sight,
    Yet love hath the power of raising.

Sweet Philomel sits on the linden green,
    Her notes melodiously blending,
And as to my soul her song pierceth e'en,
    My soul once more is distending.

——◆•◆•◆——

Which flower I love, I cannot discover;
    This grief doth impart.
In every calyx I search like a lover,
    And seek a heart.

The flowers smell sweet in the sun's setting splendor,
    The nightingale sings.
I seek for a heart that like my heart is tender,
    And like it springs.

The nightingale sings; his sweet song, void of gladness,
    Comes home to my breast;
We're both so oppress'd and heavy with sadness,
    So sad and oppress'd.

———•••———

Sweet May hath come to love us,
    Flowers, trees, their blossoms don;
And through the blue heavens above us
    The rosy clouds move on.

The nightingales are singing
    On leafy perch aloft;
The snowy lambs are springing
    In clover green and soft.

I cannot be singing and springing,
    Ill in the grass I lie;
I hear a distant ringing,
    And dream of days gone by.

———•••———

Softly through my spirit ring
    Blissful tones loved dearly,
Sound, thou little song of spring,
    Echoing far and clearly.

Sound, till thou the home com'st nigh
    Of the violet tender;
And when thou a rose dost spy,
    Say, my love I send her.

With the rose the butterfly's deep in love,
    A thousand times hovering round,
But round himself, all tender like gold,
    The sun's sweet ray is hovering found.

With whom is the rose herself in love?
    An answer I'd fain receive.
Is it the singing nightingale?
    Is it the silent star of eve?

I know not with whom the rose is in love,
    But every one love I:
The rose, the nightingale, sun's sweet ray,
    The star of eve and butterfly...

"The nightingale appear'd the first,
    And as her melody she sang,
The apple into blossom burst,
    To life the grass and violets sprang.

"She her own bosom then did bite,
    Her red blood flow'd, and from the blood
A beauteous rose tree came to light,
    To whom she sings in loving mood.

"That blood atones for, to this day,
     Us birds within the forest here;
Yet when the rose song dies away,
     Will all the wood too disappear."

Thus to his youthful brood doth speak
     The sparrow in his oaken nest;
His mate pips while she trims her beak,
     And proudly sits and looks her best.

She is a homely wife and kind,
     Broods well, and ne'er is seen to pout;
The father makes his children find
     Pastime in studying things devout.

from The Book of Songs

HEINRICH HEINE

If the nightingales knew how ill
    And worn with woe I be,
They would cheerily carol and trill,
    And all bring joy to me.

To The Nightingale

Anne Home Hunter

Why from these shades, sweet bird of eve,
     Art thou to other regions wildly fled?
Thy pensive song would oft my cares relieve,
     Thy melancholy softness oft would shed
Peace on my weary soul: return again,
Return, and, sadly sweet, in melting notes complain.

At the still hour I'll come alone,
     And listen to thy love-lorn plaintive lay;
Or when the moon beams o'er yon mossy stone,
     I'll watch thy restless wing from spray to spray,
And when the swelling cadence slow shall rise,
I'll join the harmony with low and murm'ring sighs.

Oh, simple bird! where art thou flown?
     What distant woodland now receives thy nest?
What distant echo answers to thy moan,
     What distant thorn supports thy aching breast?
Whoe'er can feel thy misery like me,
Or pay thee for thy song with such sad sympathy?

from The Revolt of Islam

PERCY BYSSHE SHELLEY

I have heard friendly sounds from many a tongue
    Which was not human—the lone nightingale
Has answered me with her most soothing song,
    Out of her ivy bower, when I sate pale
    With grief, and sighed beneath . . .

Song

CHRISTINA ROSSETTI

When I am dead, my dearest,
    Sing no sad songs for me;
Plant thou no roses at my head,
    Nor shady cypress tree:
Be the green grass above me
    With showers and dewdrops wet;
And if thou wilt, remember,
    And if thou wilt, forget.

I shall not see the shadows,
    I shall not feel the rain;
I shall not hear the nightingale
    Sing on, as if in pain:
And dreaming through the twilight
    That doth not rise nor set,
Haply I may remember,
    And haply may forget.

The Nightingale's Nest

John Clare

Up this green woodland-ride let's softly rove,
And list the nightingale—she dwells just here.
Hush! let the wood-gate softly clap, for fear
The noise might drive her from her home of love;
For here I've heard her many a merry year—
At morn, at eve, nay, all the live-long day,
As though she lived on song. This very spot,
Just where that old-man's-beard all wildly trails
Rude arbours o'er the road, and stops the way—
And where that child its blue-bell flowers hath got,
Laughing and creeping through the mossy rails—
There have I hunted like a very boy,
Creeping on hands and knees through matted thorn
To find her nest, and see her feed her young.
And vainly did I many hours employ:
All seemed as hidden as a thought unborn.
And where those crimping fern-leaves ramp among
The hazel's under-boughs, I've nestled down,
And watched her while she sung; and her renown
Hath made me marvel that so famed a bird
Should have no better dress than russet brown.
Her wings would tremble in her ecstasy,
And feathers stand on end, as 'twere with joy,
And mouth wide open to release her heart
Of its out-sobbing songs. The happiest part
Of summer's fame she shared, for so to me
Did happy fancies shapen her employ;
But if I touched a bush, or scarcely stirred,
All in a moment stopped. I watched in vain:

The timid bird had left the hazel bush,
And at a distance hid to sing again.
Lost in a wilderness of listening leaves,
Rich Ecstasy would pour its luscious strain,
Till envy spurred the emulating thrush
To start less wild and scarce inferior songs;
For while of half the year Care him bereaves,
To damp the ardour of his speckled breast;
The nightingale to summer's life belongs,
And naked trees, and winter's nipping wrongs,
Are strangers to her music and her rest.
Her joys are evergreen, her world is wide—
Hark! there she is as usual—let's be hush—
For in this black-thorn clump, if rightly guessed,
Her curious house is hidden. Part aside
These hazel branches in a gentle way,
And stoop right cautious 'neath the rustling boughs,
For we will have another search to day,
And hunt this fern-strewn thorn-clump round and round;
And where this reeded wood-grass idly bows,
We'll wade right through, it is a likely nook :
In such-like spots, and often on the ground,
They'll build, where rude boys never think to look—
Aye, as I live! her secret nest is here,
Upon this white-thorn stump! I've searched about
For hours in vain. There! put that bramble by—
Nay, trample on its branches and get near.
How subtle is the bird! she started out,
And raised a plaintive note of danger nigh,
Ere we were past the brambles; and now, near
Her nest, she sudden stops—as choking fear,
That might betray her home. So even now
We'll leave it as we found it: safety's guard

Of pathless solitudes shall keep it still.
See there! she's sitting on the old oak bough,
Mute in her fears ; our presence doth retard
Her joys, and doubt turns every rapture chill.
Sing on, sweet bird! may no worse hap befall
Thy visions, than the fear that now deceives.
We will not plunder music of its dower,
Nor turn this spot of happiness to thrall;
For melody seems hid in every flower,
That blossoms near thy home. These harebells all
Seem bowing with the beautiful in song ;
And gaping cuckoo-flower, with spotted leaves,
Seems blushing of the singing it has heard.
How curious is the nest; no other bird
Uses such loose materials, or weaves
Its dwelling in such spots : dead oaken leaves
Are placed without, and velvet moss within,
And little scraps of grass, and, scant and spare,
What scarcely seem materials, down and hair;
For from men's haunts she nothing seems to win.
Yet Nature is the builder, and contrives
Homes for her children's comfort, even here;
Where Solitude's disciples spend their lives
Unseen, save when a wanderer passes near
That loves such pleasant places. Deep adown,
The nest is made a hermit's mossy cell.
Snug lie her curious eggs in number five,
Of deadened green, or rather olive brown;
And the old prickly thorn-bush guards them well.
So here we'll leave them, still unknown to wrong,
As the old woodland's legacy of song.

LOVE

Laüstic

MARIE DE FRANCE

I shall tell you an adventure
about which the Bretons made a lai.
Laüstic was the name, I think,
they gave it in their land.
In French it is *rossignol*,
and *nightingale* in proper English.
At Saint-Malo, in that country,
there was a famous city.
Two knights lived there,
they both had strong houses.
From the goodness of the two barons
the city acquired a good name.
One had married a woman
wise, courtly, handsome;
she set a wonderfully high value on herself,
within the bounds of custom and usage.
The other was a bachelor,
well known among his peers
for bravery and great valor;
he delighted in living well.
He jousted often, spent widely
and gave out what he had.
He also loved his neighbor's wife;
he asked her, begged her so persistently,
and there was such good in him,
that she loved him more than anything,
as much for the good that she heard in him
as because he was close by.
They loved each other discreetly and well,

concealed themselves and took care
that they weren't seen
or disturbed or suspected.
And they could do this well enough
since their dwellings were close,
their houses were next door,
and so were their rooms and their towers;
there was no barrier or boundary,
except a high wall of dark stone.
From the rooms where the lady slept,
if she went to the window
she could talk to her love
on the other side, and he to her,
and they could exchange their possessions,
by tossing and throwing them.
There was scarcely anything to disturb them,
they were both quite at ease;
except that they couldn't come together
completely for their pleasure,
for the lady was closely guarded
when her husband was in the country.
Yet they always managed,
whether at night or in the day,
to be able to talk together;
no one could prevent
their coming to the window
and seeing each other there.
For a long time they loved each other,
until one summer
when the woods and the meadows were green
and the orchards blooming.
The little birds, with great sweetness,
were voicing their joy above the flowers.

It is no wonder if he understands them,
he who has love to his desire.
I'll tell you the truth about the knight:
he listened to them intently,
and to the lady on the other side,
both with words and looks.
At night, when the moon shone
when her lord was in bed,
she often rose from his side
and wrapped herself in a cloak.
She went to the window
because of her lover, who, she knew,
was leading the same life,
awake most of the night.
Each took pleasure in the other's sight
since they could have nothing more;
but she got up and stood there so often
that her lord grew angry
and began to question her, to ask
why she got up and where she went.
"My lord," the lady answered him,
"there is no joy in this world
like hearing the nightingale sing.
That's why I stand there.
It sounds so sweet at night
that it gives me great pleasure;
it delights me so and I so desire it
that I cannot close my eyes."
When her lord heard what she said
he laughed in anger and ill will.
He set his mind on one thing:
to trap the nightingale.
There was no valet in his house

that he didn't set to making traps, nets, or snares,
which he then had placed in the orchard;
there was no hazel tree or chestnut
where they did not place a snare or lime
until they trapped and captured him.
When they had caught the nightingale,
they brought it, still alive, to the lord.
He was very happy when he had it;
he came to the lady's chambers.
"Lady," he said, "where are you?
Come here! Speak to us!
I have trapped the nightingale
that kept you awake so much.
From now on you can lie in peace:
he will never again awaken you."
When the lady heard him,
she was so sad and angry.
She asked her lord for the bird
but he killed it out of spite,
he broke its neck in his hands—
too vicious an act—
and threw the body on the lady;
her shift was stained with blood,
a little, on her breast.
Then he left the room.
The lady took the little body;
she wept hard and cursed
those who betrayed the nightingale,
who made the traps and snares,
for they took great joy from her.
"Alas," she said, "Now I must suffer.
I won't be able to get up at night
or go and stand in the window

where I used to see my love.
I know one thing for certain:
he'd think I was pretending.
I must decide what to do about this.
I shall send him the nightingale and relate the adventure."
In a piece of samite,
embroidered in gold and writing,
she wrapped the little bird.
She called one of her servants,
charged him with her message,
and sent him to her love.
He came to the knight,
greeted him in the name of the lady,
related the whole message to him,
and presented the nightingale.

When everything had been told and revealed to the knight,
after he had listened well,
he was very sad about the adventure,
but he wasn't mean or hesitant.
He had a small vessel fashioned,
with no iron or steel in it;
it was all pure gold and good stones,
very precious and very dear;
the cover was very carefully attached.
He placed the nightingale inside
and then he had the casket sealed—
he carried it with him always.

This adventure was told,
it could not be concealed for long.
The Bretons made *lai* about it
which men call *The Nightingale*.

Sonnet CII

William Shakespeare

My love is strengthen'd, though more weak in seeming;
I love not less, though less the show appear:
That love is merchandized whose rich esteeming
The owner's tongue doth publish everywhere.
Our love was new and then but in the spring
When I was wont to greet it with my lays,
As Philomel in summer's front doth sing
And stops her pipe in growth of riper days:
Not that the summer is less pleasant now
Than when her mournful hymns did hush the night,
But that wild music burthens every bough
And sweets grown common lose their dear delight.
   Therefore like her I sometime hold my tongue,
   Because I would not dull you with my song.

from The Second Dayes Lamentation of the Affectionate Shepheard

RICHARD BARNFIELD

I have a pleasant noted nightingale,
That sings as sweetly as the silver swan,
Kept in a cage of bone as white as whale,
Which I with singing of Philemon wan:
Her shalt thou have, and all I have beside,
If thou wilt be my boy, or els my bride.

from Sonnets

JOHN MILTON

O Nightingale, that on yon bloomy Spray
Warbl'st at eve, when all the Woods are still,
Thou with fresh hope the Lover's heart dost fill,
While the jolly hours lead on propitious May,
Thy liquid notes that close the eye of Day,
First heard before the shallow Cucoo's bill
Portend success in love; O if Jove's will
Have linked that amorous power to thy soft lay,
Now timely sing, ere the rude Bird of Hate
Foretell my hopeless doom in some Grove nigh:
As thou from year to year hast sung too late
For my relief; yet hadst no reason why,
    Whether the Muse, or Love call thee his mate,
    Both them I serve, and of their train am I.

from The Spanish Student

HENRY WADSWORTH LONGFELLOW

How slowly through the lilac-scented air
Descends the tranquil moon! Like thistle-down
The vapory clouds float in the peaceful sky;
And sweetly from yon hollow vaults of shade
The nightingales breathe out their souls in song.
And hark! what songs of love, what soul-like sounds,
Answer them from below!

from The Masque of Pandora

HENRY WADSWORTH LONGFELLOW

Let us go forth from this mysterious place.
The garden walks are pleasant at this hour;
The nightingales among the sheltering boughs
Of populous and many-nested trees
Shall teach me how to woo thee, and shall tell me
By what resistless charms or incantations
They won their mates.